MW01049670

Classroom Management for Substitute Teachers

by S. Harold Collins

Illustrations by
Kathy Kifer Howell

A Breath of Fresh Air

Garlic Press

100 HILLVIEW LANE NO. 2 EUGENE OREGON 97401

Copyright © 1982 by Stanley H. Collins
All rights strictly reserved.

Contents

First Student: Better watch out. Our class is ROWDY.

Second Student: Naaww!

Several Students: (in unison) Yeesss.

Second Student: (in low voice) Maybe when it comes to substitutes.

Sound familiar? If you are not prepared for a crew like this, your substitute teaching experiences will be less than satisfying.

Management provides elementary Substitute Teachers a basis to manage the classroom and to teach effectively.

Members of the education community—teacher training institutions, administrators, regular classroom teachers, and Substitute Teachers—have a distinct opportunity to influence the substitute teaching role and to provide it a focus which will strengthen the professional identity and teaching effectiveness of Substitute Teachers.

Teacher Training Institutions

Teacher training institutions significantly influence the quality of teaching professionals entering the classroom. Training institutions are responsible not only for training teacher candidates, but for increasing the teaching effectiveness of educators who seek post-graduate experiences. Yet the overwhelming focus of training institutions has been upon training for the regular classroom teaching role. The substitute teaching role, tending to be a less identifiable and a less visible teaching role, has received little attention.

Teacher training institutions need to realize their training responsibility to roles which are not as traditional as the regular classroom teaching role, but which are nevertheless required for the conduct of daily education.

When training institutions decline attention to an indispensable teaching role, they withhold a status of legitimacy for that role. In the instance of the substitute teaching role, an absence of legitimacy discourages teachers from substituting and encourages other teaching professionals, students, and parents to neglect and often malign that teaching role.

Institutions which act to legitimize the substitute teaching role act to benefit the teachers they train and the quality of education those teachers provide students. Teachers trained to substitute can choose substitute teaching as a viable job role alone or as a job role which is an intermediate step to a regular classroom position. In either instance, training institutions provide a broader placement opportunity for their candidates. And in a job market which varies with population trends and public financing, flexibility as an educator is an aid to employment.

Public education is not expected to stop, closing a classroom because a teacher is absent. Every school day should be considered valuable. Trained teaching professionals must be prepared to assume appropriate roles whether by the distinguishing title of regular classroom teacher or Substitute Teacher to assure that continued value. The public should expect nothing less and teacher training institutions should conduct their programs to assure nothing less.

Let me accent substitute teaching professionals in my metropolitan area. The population of my area is about 200,000 people. It is a university town. A survey of Substitute Teachers was conducted by our local Teacher Center. Thirty-one percent of those who responded indicated that their first teaching experience was that of a Substitute Teacher. I find that statistic interesting in light of the complete absence of teacher training programs for Substitute Teachers in my state. The university in my city is providing no training for a teaching role that a sizeable portion of its graduates assume as their first teaching experience.

A second survey, by my local education association, asked its members if they had been a Substitute Teacher. Nearly 50% of those responding indicated that they had.

Administrators

If teacher training institutions can provide the professional training needed to be an effective Substitute Teacher, school districts can provide an emphasis which integrates the substitute teaching role and the professionally trained Substitute Teacher into district teaching goals. Central office administrators and building administrators must provide an atmosphere which accepts substitute teaching as an important component of district education. That atmosphere certainly must embrace the legitimacy of the substitute teaching role, clearly stating how Substitute Teachers are expected to support and further the district's educational goals and objectives.

Central office administrators provide the 'paper' rational and the basis for the integration of Substitute Teachers into the

district education goals. Individual building administrators provide the 'real' measure for Substitute Teaching effectiveness. It is up to the building administrator to foster an atmosphere which integrates the Substitute Teacher into normal, daily routines. The tone set by the building administrator influences the regular classroom teachers' regard for Substitutes, as well as the regard students have for Substitute Teachers. When a building has been guided by its administration to be supportive and accepting of Substitute Teachers, daily operations proceed fluidly with minimal loss to student engaged time, and minimal administrative and teacher energy is diverted to students who take advantage of their regular classroom teacher's absence.

Central administrators need to look at both the numerical use of Substitute Teachers and the fiscal requirements for a Substitute Teacher program. Again by local example, consider these figures. In my school district for the 1980-81 school year, Substitute Teachers served 12,034 teaching days at an expense to the district of about $625,000.

The average classroom teacher needed a Substitute Teacher ten days during the school year. Those ten days partially reflected contractual categories, but more significantly reflected my district's desire to have its teachers participate in curriculum development—and as such reflected release time.

Any number of programs in my school district receives less funding than the amount spent on Substitute Teachers. Yet Substitute Teacher funding reflects no attempt to account for the teaching competencies or teaching expectation that my district wishes its Substitute Teachers to possess, let alone to pursue.

Regular Classroom Teachers

Regular classroom teachers are the third link providing the substitute teaching role a greater definition and a greater teaching scope. Teacher training institutions have done the training. District administrators have clarified performance expectations and have integrated Substitute Teachers into curriculum goals and objectives. And now, regular classroom teachers must select appropriate Substitute Teachers for daily assignment.

If both the central office administrators and building administrators have established a clear role for the Substitute Teacher, identifying teaching expectations and standards, then regular classroom teachers should seek to support Substitute Teachers who: work well with students, work well in special environments, and can teach specialized programs. Regular classroom teachers, in accordance with any policies established by administrative criteria, should make every effort to identify Substitute Teachers who work well in their specific classrooms and make every effort to return those Substitute Teachers to their classrooms as situations arise. The classroom teacher who works in this fashion assures that planned learning will continue, that administrators will not be plagued with student discipline problems, and that other staff members can depend upon a particular Substitute Teacher to reinforce building procedures and policies.

Last school year my local district employed about 1200 full-time equivalent teachers who accrued 12,034 absences due to illness, inservice, etc. The average classroom teacher was absent ten days during a school year of 178 actual teaching days. While ten days—two weeks—is not too significant if those days are taken one-at-a-time throughout the year, ten days per teacher does have an impact. When those absences occur in blocks of several days, students are loosing educational opportunities. Planned curriculum is at least interrupted, if not totally neglected, unless the assigned Substitute Teacher is capable of picking up from yesterday and providing the continuity necessary until the regular classroom teacher returns tomorrow, the next day, or the next week.

Substitute Teachers

Substitute teachers must assume an active and an animated teaching role. That teaching role will be more successful if administrators and regular classroom teachers are supportive and if teacher institutions provide proper training for the substitute teaching role.

A challenge not only exists for Substitute Teachers to influence their teaching peers to provide a supportive teaching environment and to influence institutions to train for the substitute teaching role, but for Substitute Teachers to model effective teaching despite any present lack of support or training. Substitute Teachers should expect to teach. They must be prepared to step mid-stride into any classroom situation, gain the confidence and cooperation of students, and provide a meaningful learning experience.

Teacher Training Institutions should:

- Identify effective substitute teaching skills.
- Provide specialized training for the substitute teaching role to teacher candidates and to teacher graduates.
- Present substitute teaching to all teacher candidates as a viable teaching role.

Administrators should:

- Clarify district goals and expectations for Substitute Teachers.
- Provide services to Substitute Teachers equivalent to those offered to other staff members.
- Provide a building plan which considers the Substitute Teacher as an integral part of the building education process.
- Provide administrative support in time of conflict or need.

Regular Classroom Teachers should:

- Seek to identify Substitute Teachers who work well with children, work well in a particular building setting, can teach curriculum as prescribed by special needs, methods, or approaches.
- Seek to return effective Substitute Teachers to the classroom.
- Consider Substitute Teachers as peers.
- Prepare students for the presence of Substitute Teachers.

Substitute Teachers should:

- Be prepared to maintain continuity in planned curriculum.
- Prepare and teach lessons of their own creation when the situation warrants.
- Communicate with absent teachers and all building staff members.
- Seek to influence greater respect for the substitute teaching role.
- Operate within the stated goals and objectives of a particular school district.
- Reinforce individual building plans.

CHARACTERISTICS OF THE SUBSTITUTE TEACHING ROLE

Adaptability

The ability to deal with change, and to do so comfortably, is the most striking characteristic that distinguishes the substitute teaching role from other teaching roles. Regular classroom teachers, indeed, deal with change, but their control through planning is not a distinction that Substitute Teachers share.

To function well, Substitute Teachers must be adaptable to constantly changing surroundings, environments, and people. They must be prepared to assume a teaching situation at the ring of a phone. They must be able to tolerate confusion and bring from it an order that will quell chaos and reinforce learning.

Substitute Teachers must be able to teach a range of grades. They must be able to teach a variety of curriculum, many based on specialized techniques. They must be able not only to accommodate a variety of student personalities, but a variety of personalities which compose a building staff. They must be able to uphold building policies as well as district goals and objectives. They must be able to fulfill all of these tasks and realize that their ability to adapt and accommodate each is a key to their success.

I often think of the Substitute Teacher as a chameleon. We must be teaching professionals comfortable with constantly

changing conditions, yet teaching professionals consistent in our effect on student learning. The adaptability required of us is a worthy quality to acquire and to perfect.

Because we must be adaptable, I think Substitute Teachers gain an ''all-seeing'' perspective of their local education process that few administrators or regular classroom teachers acquire. Substitute Teachers are in more classrooms than perhaps any district person. They encounter and use a greater range of teaching techniques than perhaps any other district person. They have as great a feeling for the overall, harmonious workings of the district as does any administrator. It is the Substitute Teacher who knows the morale in the buildings as well as the morale and energy of central office people.

The opportunity to gain this ''all-seeing'' ability is excellent for those teachers who use substitute teaching as a route to a regular classroom teaching position or who use substituting as a way to test the waters before making a final commitment to a specific teaching role. They are able to observe district education in its many settings and with its many applications. They can witness a cross-section of district teachers, they can perfect skills that only practice will firm, they can identify settings and people

the "All-Seer"

Time

they would rather be a part of, and they can be closer to position openings when they occur.

From a personal basis, the most attractive feature of substitute teaching is the control it allows me of my own time. I do not take my job home with me as constantly as do regular classroom teachers. I must find time for planning, but not to the extent of the regular classroom teacher. I am not harnessed by grading, conferences, staff meetings, and any number of cosmetic preparations that regular classroom teachers must be willing to assume. Please do not think that I as a Substitute Teacher do not assume these tasks—I do in appropriate settings. The substitute teaching role requires an intense concentration during school hours, but compensates with a slacking of duty after school hours. Because my out of school hours are not in demand as those of the regular classroom teacher, I find that I am able to pursue interests that as a regular classroom teacher I would not have time to pursue.

In this section...

Adaptability

- Substitute Teachers teach a variety of curriculum.
- Substitute Teachers teach a wide range of grade levels.
- Substitute Teachers accommodate a variety of student personalities.
- Substitute Teachers uphold individual building policies and procedures.
- Substitute Teachers teach to district goals and objectives.

All-Seer

- Substitute Teachers see more classrooms than most teachers or administrators.
- Substitute Teachers encounter a greater range of curriculum techniques than most teachers or administrators.
- Substitute Teachers see a broader view of the district's overall workings than most regular classroom teachers or administrators.

Control of Time

- Demands while great in the classroom are not as intense outside the workday.
- Pursuit of personal interests is more feasible.

DECISION MAKING, TEACHING, AND MANAGEMENT

Decision Making

Teaching Role

T he decisions that Substitute Teachers must make are incredible. You must make key judgments quickly, after processing what little information may be available. The speed of decision making is unparalleled. Regular classroom teachers, because they have time to observe their students and time to consult curriculum materials, make decisions not only as a result of more information, but greater time in which to consider alternatives.

You as a Substitute Teacher must make decisions from limited alternatives, time, and information. Those decisions begin as you enter the school building. You immediately begin processing information—the people you meet, their friendliness as a measure of respect and help, the building and classroom procedures that you must know to make everyone's day 'normal,' how the students view your presence, how the absent teacher views your presence, ad infinitum.

By the time you reach the classroom, further decisions await: What are you going to teach? How are you going to teach what the regular classroom teacher has requested? Do you follow their plans completely? Or can you deviate?

Your decisions must be based on a clear understanding of the substitute teaching role. You have been trained to teach. And you are in that classroom to teach. Your prime teaching responsibility is to continue the curriculum planned by the absent teacher. That means you must be able to pick up from yesterday's assignment and conduct a lesson which will allow the regular classroom teacher to continue smoothly tomorrow or the next day. No easy task! You must be prepared to maintain the continuity established by the lesson planning of the absent teacher. You must be able to step mid-stride into planned lessons, and present the desired material in such a fashion that the absent teacher can resume the next sequential step upon return.

Teaching in this way, once again, accents the quality of adaptability. In this instance, the adaptability is sophisticated. It presupposes that you are familiar with the curriculum materials and objectives and know how best to present them to the class. Whether the content is math, science, or reading, you are expected to adapt to the content.

The primary substitute teaching role is to teach for continuity. Several secondary teaching roles are appropriate, also: teaching to provide new experiences, and teaching to reinforce existing skills. These secondary teaching roles often prove a necessity when lesson plans do not exist or when they are not clear. They also prove necessary when continuation of a requested lesson is inappropriate or is too difficult. It is no shame to assume a secondary teaching role when a Substitute Teacher is not prepared, ill prepared, or unable to piece together the sequential steps necessary for the best possible lesson presentation.

In instances when continuity cannot or should not be attempted, Substitute Teachers must be prepared to teach lessons on their own. This requirement prompts a Substitute Teacher to develop a variety of lessons which can either provide students with a new experience or which reinforce skills appropriate to a particular level.

Being thoroughly prepared to teach for continuity, to provide new experiences, or to reinforce appropriate skills are significant components of classroom management. When students must respond to competently presented content, their energies are less likely to be channelled into behaviors which are annoying or distracting. Perfecting content presentations and deliveries are important facets to managing a classroom.

Management

Decision Making

- Placement in varied surroundings requires constant decision making based upon immediate observations and available information.
- Decisions must be made relative to:
  - Students
  - Staff
  - Curriculum
  - Building policies and practices.

Teaching Role

- Teach to maintain a continuity in lesson plans of the regular classroom teacher.
- Teach to provide new experiences to students.
- Teach to reinforce skills appropriate to competency levels.

Classroom Management

- Classroom management is closely related to how well a Substitute Teacher:
  - Can make decisions,
  - Can teach for continuity, for new experiences, and for reinforcement of acquired skills.

BEING-IN-CHARGE

Standards and Values

Subject matter preparedness and delivery are important to classroom management. But before you can present subject matter, you must establish yourself as **being-in-charge** of the classroom.

I can identify five components that, in ever changing proportions and accents, establish the Substitute Teacher as **being-in-charge** and **managing** of the classroom. The first two components require a constant introspection. A Substitute Teacher must know enough about themself to identify and to embrace certain standards and values as those standards and values apply to social living, to communication among people, and to learning. From these foundation bricks describing their person, a Substitute Teacher must be able to develop a teaching style which reinforces their beliefs.

For the Substitute Teacher, developing a teaching style poses a difficulty not experienced by regular classroom teachers. While regular classroom teachers must certainly be adaptable to their school setting and student population, Substitute Teachers must be many times more adaptable, since they meet many more teaching situations and students. It is because of this greater requirement for adaptability that Substitute Teachers have difficulty identifying a teaching style which is at all consistent and not, seemingly, schizophrenic.

I speak of these first two components are requiring constant introspection. I see this introspection as a self-checking mechanism to adapt style to personal standards and values. I also see a substitute teaching style as requiring many more instructional and management techniques to its composition than the teaching style of the regular classroom teacher. Those techniques which compose the style require constant polish and instant use wholly dependent upon the classroom that a Substitute Teacher enters each day.

If you have identified your standards and values and have honed your style accordingly, you affirm your substitute character. The confidence that your character projects is then mirrored to the students you meet.

The third component of being-in-charge is what I refer

Personal Teaching Style

"Power of the Unknown"

Rapport

to as "The Power of the Unknown." Think for a moment. If you were a student, how would you respond to a Substitute Teacher whom you see for the first time a few moments before the morning bell? Until that person reveals themself by words and actions, you have no way of knowing what your limits—behavior or learning—are. You will be more attentive to this new person until you can identify why you either want to cooperate with them or give them a hard time. That person is an unknown quanitity.

I think this *power* that resides in being an *unknown* person is a distinct benefit to you as a Substitute Teacher. Until you reveal yourself, students do not have a basis upon which they can make judgments of cooperation or resistance.

The bell has rung and you now have the attention of your students. I find that these first few moments provide a major influence upon how the remaining hours of the day will unfold. The *power of the unknown* has at least momentarily provided you the opportunity to establish how the day can proceed. If your mere presence provides a momentum for establishing what you expect and who you are, how do you extend control past these first few introductory minutes? Component four, *rapport.*

I would like to take these first four components of being-in-charge and use them in what I call an *"opener."* I have a somewhat standard procedure I use to begin a school day. This opener provides students with information which they need and gathers for me information I need to conduct a meaningful day. Here is a patter that closely approximates how I begin taking charge:

> *(Bell)* "All right. I would like everyone to sit down and give me their attention up here. *(Pause)* Great. Thank You.
>
> "I need to tell you several things and to ask several things of you. . .here we go. My name is Mr. Collins. I have the chance to be with you today and I am looking forward to an interesting day.
>
> "I don't know exactly what happened to your regular teacher, whether he/she is ill or had to go somewhere. But whatever the reason, as I said, I have a chance to be with you today.
>
> "You're going to find out that I don't do things exactly like your regular teacher. But I think you will enjoy today. I have brought some interesting activities that I would like to share with you as the day goes on. It all depends on you. If I can get your cooperation and help, the day will go well."

To this point I have told them what I know about their teacher, that I will be there all day, and that I do not do things exactly like their regular teacher ("But that's not how our regular teacher does it."). I have also let them know that I have "brought

some interesting things'' with me. This entire presentation is given congenially, but firmly.

I must at this point gather information from them. This is my chance to see how they will respond to me. I need to find out the morning procedures: lunch count, duties, absences, pledge, etc.

> "I don't know all of your procedures. Can someone tell me by raising a hand about. . . . ''

I am beginning to ask for their help and I am establishing that I like hands raised to talk. I believe that students like to help, even Substitute Teachers. So I make an effort to ask for their help. In a group appeal, you are not likely to get misinformation. And in asking for their help, I am getting them to work and to participate with me. This is a low level, but effective, technique to gain their trust and support, and to build rapport.

Occasionally I will get one or two individual responses which are obviously not productive to the rapport I am trying to establish. The *power of the unkown* is still with me to stop inappropriate remarks (which can be early signs of inappropriate behavior).

> "I'm sorry, remarks like that aren't appreciated! If you have something to say, it had better be a good remark. Otherwise I don't care to hear it. I'm generally a happy person and I like to stay that way. But remarks like yours can make me mad. And there is no use making me mad, I can get mean.''

By responding with a remark like this to a particular student, you deal with one student, but warn every student. You are reinforcing your classroom expectations for student behavior and for a learning environment.

Any type of brief exchange that you can have with students helps to establish you as a personality and what you expect as a teacher. To help extend rapport further, I continue:

> "I don't know everyone here. I met a few of you before school. So I won't have to go around all day saying, 'Hey, you,' let me read a name. If I call your name, just raise your hand.
> "Michelle. . . . Hi, Michelle."
> "Jason is where? . . . Howdy, Jason."

I must be honest. I have great difficulty remembering names. As one student tells me their name, I have forgotten it when a second student tells me theirs. But the significance of this exercise is to make contact with students individually. When they let you know who they are, your eye contact and a smile go a long way toward getting cooperation and toward building rapport. They think you know who they are, once you have called their name, and that you will remember them specifically. The importance here is that they have given you something, their name. They think you will remember it—and you will as the day goes on—and that your eye contact, smile, and comment to them is an extension of friendship—which it is. The key is "they think." If you can get them to think positively about you, much of the inappropriate, testing behavior kids are so noted for can be eliminated or greatly reduced. Checking inappropriate behavior early or before it begins through a simple interaction like this is important to classroom management.

How you project being-in-charge carries past the "opener." Please bear in mind that the opener is a prime vehicle which can establish your teaching potential, and how well you establish communications with the students. Once past the opener, the fifth component of being-in-charge is available: *making yourself the reinforcer.*

Short time-spans when you can direct the students' attention to something you have, something which is high-interest, can serve as a reinforcement for their conduct. You are not only reinforcing behavior, but adding to the Substitute Teacher-student rapport. You can use yourself as the key to this. I find that establishing myself early as the reinforcer works best, right after or as a part of the opener. Here is a quick activity I use immediately after I have satisfied roll and first of the morning chores. I call it "How many of you. . . ."

> "I would like to find out more about you people. I have here a list of questions I would like to ask. You can answer these questions by raising a hand. For instance:

the Reinforcer

"How many of you like to stay up late? Aw, a lot of hands went up.

"How many of you are the oldest child in your family? The youngest? The only?

"How many of you have flown in an airplane?

". . .have been on a farm?

". . .have a pet?"

I like to depart from hand raising and zero in on a specific child. Doing this highlights that child's response and allows, once again, one-to-one contact. Here is how I depart and then return to my script:

"How many of you make your own breakfast? Who made their breakfast this morning? *(pick a child)* What did you have? *(response)* Interesting. *(pick a child)* Who made something different? *(response)."*

"How many of you love chocolate ice cream? *(to a child)* What's your favorite? *(response)* *(to another)* And what's yours?"

You can weave in and out from your list, departing to ask for a response, each time accenting a different child. In this way, if you can also remember a few names, the students begin to respond to your cues, your personality, and they begin to sense that the difference which characterizes you, the Substitute Teacher, is a desirable quality (or pay-off, if you must) for them.

The list that I read from contains a wide variety of questions. It must, since I must be prepared to use it for a wide span of ages. I do not read every question, I am selective, choosing appropriate ones for my daily situation. I constantly add to the list to keep it fresh.

The opportunity to use yourself as the reinforcer has prime application for other time-spans. For instance, during dead moments: just before recess, as a transition between curriculum presentations, just after recess or P.E. when kids are all wound-up and need calming.

Using yourself as the reinforcer allows the students to focus attention on you. You have something for them that, by their participation, channels any energy that might be used otherwise disruptively. These openers (I sometimes call them "Introductions") and filler activities also support the management of the classroom in another way. If you are able to arouse student interest through a short span activity, that interest is likely to carry over into curriculum involvement with an enthusiasm which may not have been previously present in a particular student or in an entire class.

Being-in-charge has an authoritarian ring. But the Substitute Teacher who fails to assume the controlling role in a class relinquishes classroom management. A Substitute Teacher must be quick and effective to establish their "in-charge" status. Where the regular classroom teacher has time to assess, practice, and refine their management techniques for one particular class, the Substitute Teacher must be able to process information quickly and institute on the spot management techniques. I have tried to point to five components, with teaching examples that you, the Substitute Teacher, can use to establish yourself as being-in-charge. These components are what I consider a basis for classroom management. They are considerations which focus on why you are teaching, how you can gain student interest, and how you can establish a communication bound with students.

I am not so smug as to think that classroom management does not involve other techniques or considerations. I will be more pointed later regarding classroom management rules and consequences. You will still encounter variations of inappropriate behavior no matter how well you perfect the five components I have mentioned.

In this section...

Five components for Being-in-Charge

- An awareness of personal standards and values as they apply to social living, communications, and learning.
- An affirmation of one's own personal teaching style.
- Using the "Power of the Unknown."
- An ability to establish rapport.
- Establishing yourself as the reinforcer.

WHO ARE YOU?
OR
WHY DO THEY
DO THESE THINGS
TO ME?

The nature of our teaching role which requires constant movement from classroom to classroom fosters certain student remarks and closely associated behaviors which the permanence of the regular classroom teaching situation quickly eliminates. We are prone to hear certain remarks often, and we spend more time attending to those remarks than do our regular classroom counterparts.

I would like to discuss several common remarks and two broader categories of expression as they influence teaching effectiveness and as they influence student behavior. How well we attend to these remarks and expressions reflects upon our management of the classroom.

"Our regular classroom teacher doesn't do it that way."

A simple and often effective retort is, "Well, I'm not your regular classroom teacher." A retort like this is effective if a student or several students are merely "testing" you. Many times it is all you need utter to inform students of your desire to "be-in-charge."

A retort like this, though, can alienate an entire class. And alienation provides fodder for disruptive behavior. Students often find security and regularity in the patterns provided by their regular classroom teacher. Breaking their established security, no matter how pleasant and well intentioned you are, can be difficult for them to accept. Also, radical departure from their established routine may be taken as a negation of a teacher they dearly love, so closely do they associate the procedure with the personality of their classroom teacher.

A very refined judgment you need to make each and every classroom you enter is, Can I teach best by requiring students to do things absolutely my way? Or, should I try to work within the teaching structure established for them by their regular classroom teacher? I find a personal substitute teaching style which strikes a balance. I want the students to accept my being-in-charge. But I am willing, and prefer them, to identify classroom policies and procedures familiar to them and which they will observe while I am in their classroom. I want them to be comfortable in their classroom with a new person, but a new person who expects to be in control to teach. I do not hesitate to unilaterally end regular practices which are not working well.

You need to be aware that the "We don't do it that way" remark can have an influence on your classroom management.

"I don't have to listen to you, you're just an old Substitute."

When a regular classroom teacher hears this challenge, it is "My father (or mother) said I don't have to do what you say." While I might answer, "Well, I'm not that old," and ignore the real challenge, the student is questioning my teaching role and my being-in-charge. The student has been able to generalize that he or she can manipulate me because a Substitute Teacher is not a "real" teacher. I do not hesitate to assert firmly my legitimacy as a teacher. I am also prepared to institute consequences if words or actions are directed further to disruptive behavior.

Usually this remark is uttered by a single student. The "Power of the Unknown" and rapport techniques will usually isolate this remark to individuals.

"Can I get a drink of water?. . .Can I go to the bathroom?. . . Can I. . . ."

The ultimate joy of students, it seems, is to be out of their seats, or better yet, out of the classroom as much as possible when they have a Substitute Teacher. Consequently, one of the first, and one of the most persisting, behaviors of kids is the inquiry "Can I go to the bathroom?"—library, nurse, office, get a drink, get my coat on the playground, ad infinitum.

The Substitute Teacher too often responds to these

remarks out of a sense of jeopardy: "Suppose he really does have a bladder problem?" Or . . . is sick . . . has lost her coat . . . needs water? Once students sense your leniency to their "Can I's," they become disruptive to your teaching with their petty requests. Still you do need to make individual decisions of yes or no. I have concluded that this "Can I" behavior is part of kid-ness, to get away with as much as possible. But to reduce it, as the regular classroom teacher has, requires bound setting. If the kids can not observe their normal policies in this regard, I unilaterally establish policy . . . but make individual exceptions.

Attention Getting/Power Struggles

Attention

Attention getting antics are constant. To the extent that they influence the class or influence you, they detract from classroom management. Two common forms of attention getting are: antics which seek your attention and antics which seek peer attention.

Much of the attention-getting that is directed at you is a child's way of saying to a new person, "Hello there, I want you to know I exist." They want you to interact with them. Usually this attempt at interaction is not intended to be mean or obnoxious. If you are adept, you can capitalize on this interaction to get individuals with you, building quick rapport. If interactions are obnoxious, you need to make direct statements to that effect.

Antics which seek peer attention are often harder to deal with and to extinguish. There is often a cliquishness that can form between several students who will perform for one another, and when called to task, perform against you. I find that kidding around with students who are trying to gain peer attention is often a way to reduce acting out. If I can get in on their clowning, I can then exert requests as one of the group to stop behaviors.

When I cannot ignore the needs for peer attention any further, or cannot direct that attention as I want, I must be prepared to issue and follow through with consequences.

Power Struggles

The most frustrating exchange with students occurs in a power struggle. I do not know how many times I have reminded myself NEVER argue with a student, only to find myself baited into an argument. Part of that susceptibility to baiting is the teaching need to come out on top, to be the authority.

I am getting better about power struggles. When I find myself in one, I abruptly stop participating. I also try to avoid a struggle in front of the entire class. In this situation, I show my venom to the entire class, and I provide the involved student(s) free "air time," both are to my detriment.

Extreme needs for attention and power often manifest turmoil in a student's personality that Substitute Teachers have no background information to counteract. Any communication between regular classroom teachers and Substitute Teachers which would provide the Substitute Teacher a basis for dealing with special cases is highly warranted. Yet, in the absence of this kind of communication, the Substitute Teacher must be able to head-off, minimize, or deflate student behaviors.

RULES,
CONSEQUENCES,
AND CREATIVE
ADJUSTMENTS

To this point, I have presented a broad format which can help establish you as a classroom manager. Managing the classroom begins with your educational beliefs developed into a teaching style. Managing the classroom takes into account your ability to "be-in-charge" of the classroom, to establish rapport with students, and to teach academic subjects whether from the plans of the regular classroom teacher or from the lessons you develop. Yet you cannot be an effective educator and skillful manager of the classroom without establishing rules for conduct and subsequent consequences for rule violations.

Inappropriate behavior is a problem that all educators experience in their efforts to teach children. Different teaching roles require somewhat different methods to deal with behavior which detracts from teacher effectiveness and from student academic performance. Teachers in the regular classroom teaching role can observe behavior longer, identify causal relationships, and plan to extinguish inappropriate behavior because they are daily with an assigned group of students. Substitute Teachers in their role do not have the benefit of time to observe, identify, and plan for behavior change. The substitute teaching role does not allow the element of time to view and extinguish inappropriate behavior through a prescribed and executed behavior routine. Nevertheless, the Substitute Teacher can develop a framework to deal with student behaviors.

That framework begins with a Substitute Teacher establishing classroom rules. Here are guidelines to help in establishing classroom rules:

- *Rules must be consistent with building policies*
- *Rules must be stated in specific terms*
- *Rules must be clearly stated*
- *Rules must be reasonable*
- *Rules must be enforceable*

Each classroom a Substitute Teacher enters warrants guiding rules. A Substitute Teacher must establish those rules quickly after processing what information they have gained from administrative comments, teacher communications, and, most important, the mood and composure of the students in the classroom. The Substitute Teacher can unilaterally determine and apply classroom rules. They could jointly determine and apply rules with the help of the students. The students could solely

Rules

determine and apply the rules. Or, the classroom rules already established by regular classroom teacher can be applied. No matter how rules are determined, they must be specific, clearly defined, reasonable, and enforceable.

Here is a sampling of rules Substitute Teachers might consider:

- *Follow directions the first time they are given.*
- *Keep hands, feet, objects to yourself.*
- *Use acceptable language.*
- *Ignore bad behavior of others.*
- *Stay at assigned task.*
- *Arrive on time to class.*
- *Move quietly in the classroom.*
- *Raise your hand to talk.*

A laundry list of rules will be less than fully effective. Choose four, or five at most, to apply.

In a classroom where my quickly formed impressions signal a suitability, I use an opener which involves students in establishing classroom rules. I merely state my need for establishing rules so we both (Substitute Teachers and students) know what to expect during the day. I do this in an upbeat fashion and ask students to write one or two rules on a slip of paper and hand that slip to me. I then synthesize a representative list.

No matter how you establish rules, remember: you are "in-charge." You are the bond that holds the entire process together. I have come to feel strongly that kids will put up with a lot if they like you and feel you—hence, take time to build rapport. Now, that does not mean you are out for adulation or popularity. It means kids will generally accept your rules and restraints if they have a positive feeling for you. When you are practicing the "in-charge" components I discussed earlier, you are more likely to project yourself as an acceptable personality and teacher, and thus more likely to gain their cooperation.

When you establish classroom rules, you must also establish consequences for those who choose not to follow the established rules.

Consequences must be:

- *Consistent with building practices.*
- *Clearly stated before they are enforced.*
- *Fairly administered.*
- *Consistently enforced.*
- *Reasonable.*
- *Logical in terms of misbehavior.*

Consequences

Severity

In determining your consequences, you will need to establish severity levels. Perhaps a warning is the lowest consequence and dispatch to the building administrator the most severe, with intermediate steps which remove free time, recess, or require a student to remain after school. You must determine those severity levels for yourself and execute them within the established behavior expectations of the particular school to which you are assigned.

I find that the Big Three (Being-in-charge, Rules, Consequences) need reinforcement in specific settings. Once I have invoked my in-charge character and established rules and consequences, problems that I generally encounter come from individual students. When specific students exhibit their inappropriate behaviors, yes, I can quickly administer consequences, but there are other techniques I will likely use to head off further behavior exhibitions and any definite need for consequences.

I have developed a hierarchy of simple techniques I use before I lower the boom with consequences. These techniques do

not replace consequences, but serve as simple, low level defusing attempts to head off possible misbehavior displays. They are the ounce of prevention that I administer before consequences. The hierarchy is nothing new in education, it is just an organization of simple techniques to gain an individual's cooperation.

Ignore. When possible, ignore behaviors which will extinguish when they are not reinforced by your or by peer attention.

Eye Contact. Non-verbal communication directed at the misbehaving student.

Gestures. Let a misbehaving child know of their behavior through facial reactions (frown, raised eyebrows), head movements, or directional gestures (finger to lips, hand wave).

Praise. Praise 'model behavior.'

Proximity Control. Move closer to a child who is

Hierarchy of Techniques

31

misbehaving. Move a child closer to you, or perhaps away from others who reinforce that child's behavior. Move about the room making contact with all class members.

Directed Verbal Comments. Tell the misbehaving child that you want them to change. State how they are to change and what you expect. Remind them of consequences. Reinforce occurring appropriate behavior.

Touch. Physical contact (not abuse) is both a reinforcement and a calming technique—a pat on the back, a hand on the shoulder. A firm hand on the shoulder and strong eye contact has a calming, "I mean business" effect on some students. Or take a student's hand, leading them to their seat, followed by a verbal direction.

If . . . Then. . . . This technique feeds right into my established consequences. If you do this . . . then, this happens. . . . Consequences quickly follow any repeated behavior.

Creative Adjustments

Because I personally do not expect to have a single, iron-clad response to fit every inappropriate behavior I encounter, I find that I am often creative in my application of behavioral consequences. I will often tailor a behavior plan to an individual. Here are two examples in the creative vein that I have used in warranted situations. They focus, for illustration here, about two behaviors which bother me greatly—talkouts and random movement about the classroom.

On a small slip of paper I: write the misbehaving student's name, then identify the behaviors to which he or she must attend. I walk to that student's desk and tape the slip in one corner, and say:

"I'm putting this slip here. Each time you choose to talkout, I will put a market here *(point to the word "talkout" on the slip)*. Each time you choose to wander from your seat, I will put a mark here *(point)*. For every mark you get, you will stay after school one minute."

For students who scoff and threaten to remove the slip:

"If you remove the slip you will automatically owe five minutes after school."

The creative aspect in this situation is the use of the slip. The consequences are tailored to the individual and applied through the slip of paper.

This technique works on a limited basis. It does not work at all if more than two or three students exhibit unacceptable behaviors you want to control; otherwise, the students control you, having you run from one to another delivering marks.

Suppose this same student either continues to exhibit their inappropriate behaviors or pulls something that is grossly counter to my classroom management goals. The severity of my response would increase. I might involve a parent. And I could do it in this manner:

In my state, as in many, the law requires that information be kept accessible pertaining to each student, listing parental data, phone numbers—both work and home—and emergency contact information. This information is usually kept in the office.

I have the student accompany me to the office. I ask the secretary to give me the parental information. I call the parent right there with the child in front of me, and with the knowledge of the secretary.

"Hello, Mr./Mrs./Ms. _____ ? My name is _____ . I am a Substitute Teacher today in your child's class. The regular teacher is absent today.

"I am having behavior problems with your child. . .*(state exactly)*. . .

"I am a certified teacher who has come to this class to teach. Your child is making it difficult for me to teach and is interfering with the learning of others. I hope you will agree with me that your child is here to learn. Isn't that true. . ." *(parent responds)*

"I have your child standing here in front of me at this moment. I wanted your child to know that we both have expectations for him/her. I think you will agree to that too. . ." *(elicit response)*

"Do you want to talk to your child?"

"Thank you for your support. I hope your child's day goes much better after this conversation."

The creative adjustment to this situation is parental contact with the offending child present. The consequence carried a conversation with parent, child, and Substitute Teacher involved.

I do not use this technique wantonly. It is a very effective technique, humbling to the student. I have had the entire conversation before the child, the secretary in the background, and I have phrased my statements in such a way as to get parental support.

I must say that when I use it, I make a judgment as to whether it will be the most effective technique to use. I might ask another teacher, the secretary, or the building administrator about parental concern for that child. If the student is mouthy, might lie, or if a parent might not prove supportive, I use another technique.

This technique is daring, no question! But it does not overstep my teaching bounds, and it is effective.

In writing this section, I cannot hope to address each of the many classroom management problems that Substitute Teachers will encounter. I have suggested large areas which when systematically considered will help Substitute Teachers to organize their conduct of classroom management. We all encounter many of the same classroom management problems, but it is the resolve that we each pursue which minimizes or eliminates conflicts and maximizes our teaching effectiveness. You must embellish these considerations to make them workable for the specific settings you will enter and the specific characters you will encounter.

In this section...

Rules should be:
- Consistent with building policies
- Stated in specific terms
- Clearly stated
- Reasonable
- Enforceable.

Consequences should be:
- Consistent with building practices
- Clearly stated before they are enforced
- Fairly administered
- Consistently enforced
- Reasonable
- Logical in terms of misbehavior.

Complementing Classroom Techniques
- Low level ways to defuse or head off inappropriate behavior displays (not a replacement for consequences).
- A Simple Hierarchy of Classroom Management Techniques:
  - Ignore
  - Eye Contact
  - Gestures
  - Praise
  - Proximity Control
  - Directed Verbal Comments
  - Touch
  - If...Then...

Creative Adjustment
- Tailoring consequences to specific individuals.

COMMUNICATING WITH REGULAR CLASSROOM TEACHERS

Substitute Teachers must be assertive in their job role, certainly in the classroom with students, but also outside of the classroom to communicate with their regular classroom teaching peers. The Substitute Teacher who can comfortably approach and talk to staff members about the substitute teaching role serves three ends: first, the Substitute Teacher will establish in the minds of regular classroom teachers the desire to be an effective teacher; second, the Substitute Teacher will come to understand the needs and requirements of specific schools and classrooms; and, third, the Substitute Teacher will increase their likelihood of return to a particular school and classroom.

I encourage Substitute Teachers to initiate interaction with regular classroom teachers. I remember my first fears of initiating conversations with classroom teachers. At first, I conjured the likelihood of alienating them merely by voicing my opinions and concerns. Then, to counterbalance, I imagined conversations that oozed with patronization. I quickly found that fear of alienation or the need for patronization was totally unnecessary. I generally found responses heartening. And more often I found my effort influencing procedures which included Substitute Teachers more uniformly into a school building plan. For example, here is a "lesson plan form" that a building's 5/6 grade teachers developed in response to the needs of Substitute Teachers:

LESSON PLANS FOR: _____

Teacher's Name

Welcome!

This is a _____grade class. You will find the Home Room Class list in the
folder. Before going into the lesson plans, there are some things about this
classroom and school that you should know:

1) Our school uses the Assertive Discipline® Plan. Classroom expectations
   are posted on the front board. The school rules are the same. I use
   the Assertive Discipline® in all my classes by using lots of praise
   and notes home to parents. For those who choose to not follow the rules,
   I put their name on the board which is a warning. If they continue to
   disrupt, then a check goes after the name. A behavior report should
   be left for the teacher.

2) The 5/6 grades performance group for reading and math. Please observe
   the class times precisely.

3) Room Duties are listed on the front bulletin board.

4) Fire Drills: If the fire bell goes off, your class that you have for
   the moment goes directly out back door and lines up on the soccer field.
   When you have accounted for all those that you're in charge of, then
   raise your hand.

NOW FOR THE REGULAR DAY SCHEDULE

8:20   Students may enter the room. Once in the room, they do not leave
       without your permission. Students are to be seated by the 8:30 bell.

8:30   Take attendance and lunch count. On the lunch count, you can order a
       regular lunch for $1.85 or you can order a chef salad for $1.50. Several
       students attend strings or band classes. They arrive about 8:45.

       Give about five minutes for students to share anything that is newsworthy.

9:00   Reading and Spelling. You will have a group of _____.
       These students are _____. _____
       is our regular textbook.

       DO this for today:

10:05 Dismiss from reading. Students return to homeroom.
       Ball monitors hand out the passes. You have a break during this time.
       In case of rainy day and the announcement is made to stay inside, you
       are to stay in the room for duty. Acceptable activities are posted
       in the front of the room.

10:10 Dismiss for recess.

10:25   Recess over

10:30   Dismiss for math. You will have _____ who are

         working in _____.

         Do this for today:

         All scores are recorded in % and in pencil. I allow students to correct
         their daily work and I record their scores in the grade book. Dismiss
         math at 11:15.

11:15   Home room. This is usually devoted to language art activities; especially
         writing.

         Do this today:

11:50 - 12:30 Lunch and recess. Ball monitors hand out ball cards after taking
               your class to lunch. This is your 30 minutes duty-free lunch time.

12:30   Students return to their home room to read until 1:00.

         Do this:

 2:25   Housekeepers clean the boards and sinks and everyong gets the room picked
         up, desks on the dots. Students put up their chairs and go home.
         End of Day. Whew!

         Please leave a note on how things went. Also, here are the things I want
         you to do before you leave:

         1. Papers for the day checked over, graded and recorded.
         2. Room in good order
         3. Leave a note for me telling me how things went. If there were specific
             problems or difficulties (of any kind) I'd like to know about it.

                              THANK YOU

                      _____

This "lesson plan form" is a good model. Because we Substitute Teachers travel from school to school, I was quick to leave it at subsequent schools as a tangible model that others might use or possibly modify for further use. Our mobility as teachers does provide us with a format for sharing that other teaching professionals who are bound to specific buildings do not experience.

Here is a folder that one building provides Substitute Teachers each morning when they arrive. It is very inclusive, but most of all it is concise in its statements of information.

Substitute Teacher's Handbook

*Welcome
to
McCornack School*

SICK CHILD

FIRE ALARM

FREE TIME, RAINY DAYS, ETC.

SUPPLIES—TEACHERS GUIDES—EDITIONS

FILMS—MUSIC—LIBRARY—ETC.

TEAM TEACHING—CO-OPERATIVE TEACHING—CLASSROOM CHANGES

LESSON PLAN BOOK

SPECIAL ASSIGNMENTS—SUPERVISION

CHILDREN WHO MAY NEED OR REQUIRE YOUR SPECIAL ATTENTION

CHILDREN WHO MAY BE OF HELP

SEATING CHART

ROOM RULES

DAILY CLASS SCHEDULE

ADDITIONAL INFORMATION

BUILDING PLAN

SCHOOL TIME SCHEDULE

I have shown you how two buildings provide information to Substitute Teachers and I have suggested that you circulate appropriate models to schools which lack them. Here, in addition, is a form letter that you might be able to leave, remember you can modify it to your local needs, in schools to spark heightened attention to your teaching needs and requirements.

WHEN A SUBSTITUTE TEACHER COMES IN THE DOOR

In preparing for the arrival of a substitute teacher (me), it would be very helpful if the classroom teacher would consider a "worst possible scenario" and make preparations in a way that anticipates and facilitates the substitute's task. When I walk into your school I am entering what amounts to a new culture; your help in advance can assist greatly in reducing my culture shock. The sooner I can grasp the essentials of your classroom culture the more able I am to do a productive job working with your students.

INFORMATION NEEDED:

HELP!! I got the call 20 minutes ago and I just arrived—I have 3 minutes before the class starts.

- KEY STUDENTS
- SEATING CHART
- TAKING ROLL
- REGULAR CLASS-ROOM PROCEDURES

They handed me a packet a quarter-inch thick in the office and said "the room is down the hall." Will students facilitate the class —or will someone undermine it? Is there someone I can count on to be a help or hindrance? Is the seating chart accurate enough to take roll from? In taking roll is there a special marking system—or do you want it on a separate sheet? Are there procedures the class always follows—and if so, is deviation o.k. from students' view? From the regular teacher's? (i.e., homework—correct? Hand in? Where? Late?)

- PREP PERIODS
- TEXT USED
- TEXTS LOCATION

You have four different subjects to teach just before lunch. Your prep period is the last period of the day. I've never taught here before and I don't know any of the students. I don't know what texts or materials you use with which class—and if they aren't right in front of me, I don't know where to look.

- EXPECTATIONS FOR STUDENTS

Are there rules? Are they posted? Where? Are they enforced? How? Can I get administrative support if I need it? From whom?

- SPECIAL EXCEPTIONS

What do students do if they get done with an assignment? Can students go to the lavatory? Library? Etc.? Do some leave early? Are some working on special projects? Are there special medical considerations, e.g., bee sting, other allergies, epilepsy, medication?

- WHAT WOULD YOU LIKE TO KNOW WHEN YOU RETURN?

Should I report to you? What? Behavior, who what? Lesson covered, how well? Where are supplemental materials?

I can only expect to provide a limited number of folders, or lesson plan forms, or "scenario letters" to staff members. I must also rely on verbal statements gently directed toward enhancing the substitute teaching role if I expect a building staff to prepare better for Substitute Teachers.

I have found that my statements are productive over the long run. Change does take place. And perhaps as rewarding, I do establish myself as a respectable teacher who is consistently requested to work. Communicating does have its professional benefits as it does its financial benefits.

How do you carry your communication to the absent classroom teacher you are replacing? Upon a return visit to that school, you can certainly make contact with that teacher—and should. But how do you speak to that absent teacher about your day in their classroom? First of all, I feel, as it is the responsibility of the regular classroom teacher to provide you with lesson plans, it is your responsibility to communicate in writing what went on in their classroom during your day. Yes, in some instances, you must know when to temper your comments. Yet, the minimum that you should communicate is what you did during the day, with any special attention to deviation from teacher plans.

You should always report what work you accomplished in curriculum presentation. Beyond that, you need to be tactful if you must point to student behavior or to the teacher's consideration of your teaching role.

When it comes to reporting student behavior, I often harken back to a teacher who said, "When I return, I don't want to know all the trials and tribulations you experienced." This teacher was not being flippant. When she spoke further, I understood her comment better: "I have many of the same problems, and I'm working on them." This teacher expected me to handle the problems, and expected staff, administration, and parents to support me just as they did her. Yes, she really wanted to know of significant behavior problems, but not an action-by-action recount of my day. From her example, I have developed a line of understatement that I include when the day has been difficult: "I don't imagine I experienced anything that you haven't."

I find it often necessary to comment to my absent teacher about how they can better prepare for a Substitute Teacher in the future. I may leave them a "scenario letter," I may write in understatement, or I may feel that the situation requires pointed comment.

To a teacher who left me absolutely no clues or information from which to teach, I wrote: "Although you didn't provide me with any information, I feel it is my professional responsibility to provide you with information about what I accomplished during your absence. . . ."

To a teacher who obviously took pains to provide me with information, I wrote: "Thank you for your preparation. The length to which you were willing to prepare is a great measure of my teaching success in your classroom and a large measure of how well your students adjust to my presence."

To a teacher to whom I wanted to express my concern, I wrote: "The day went pretty well. But I did have certain difficulty impressing upon your students the responsibility they each have for their own behavior. When I called students to task for inappropriate behavior, I continually experienced whining or blaming."

No matter what I write to the absent teacher, I always sign my full name and leave my phone number to "talk further, if need be." I never want a teacher to feel that they cannot respond to what I have written.

I also feel that a Substitute Teacher should communicate assertively when a situation like this arises:

I returned for a second day to this assignment. I found this note in the absent teacher's box.

> Mrs. D — Bruce and Robert decided not to cooperate during music.
> —Mrs. J
> P.S. The kids were high in general, the sub brought them 10 minutes late....

I was unable to locate the music teacher, so I wrote this note in return. I also left a copy for the absent teacher.

> Mrs. J.—I tried to locate you today. I was here Thursday and Today for Mrs. D.
> I wanted to respond to the "P.S." of your letter to Mrs. D.
> (1.) The kids were "high" p.m. for me, too.
> (2.) Mrs. D. forgot to mention your music period. Sorry, I did not intend to leave music out. Communications were just crossed up.
> Your "P.S." has the tone of blaming the "Substitute Teacher" for two problems. I hope that wasn't your intention. You deserve support and consideration in what you do. I expect to provide that support and consideration as best I can.
> —Stan Collins, Substitute Teacher

I have included this section on "Communicating with Regular Classroom Teachers" because communication is an influence on classroom management. How well you can convey your teaching needs does influence how regular classroom teachers will provide for your effectiveness in their absences.

NO
PANACEA

Educators are often lead to believe that they can be vaccinated through inservice, special curriculum presentations, seminars, and, yes, books like this for what ails them. We love to think that there are simple means, both quick and efficient, which will get us past certain perceived shortcomings.

"Aw, I need better classroom management skills. Look at Such-in-such. They do it so magnificently. Maybe I'll learn it all by talking with Such-in-such, taking a class, or by reading a book."

The facts are: Such-in-such has not acquired those magnificent skills unpracticed; and classes and books do not alone issue flawless results. Anything a teacher does perfect is done with a brute resolve and perseverence. This book is not a panacea for Substitute Teacher classroom management. It is a starting point though. You should use the suggestions here as a basis to perfect your own classroom management and teaching style.

Classroom management for Substitute Teachers requires a personal resolve to organize yourself and to work amidst others (the regular classroom teacher and the building administrator) to achieve your most effective teaching role.

GARLIC⬧PRESS ENGLISH SERIES

Straight Forward English Series

Capitalization and Punctuation #GP-032
Nouns and Pronouns #GP-033
Verbs #GP-034
Adjectives & Adverbs #GP-035

The *Straight Forward English Series* is designed to measure, teach, review, and master specific English skills: *Capitalization and Punctuation; Nouns and Pronouns; Verbs;* and, *Adjectives and Adverbs*.

Each workbook is a simple straightforward approach to learning English skills. Skills are keyed to major school textbook adoptions.

Pages are reproducible.

SUBSTITUTE TEACHING GARLIC⬧PRESS

Substitute Teacher Folder
#GP-027

Substitute Teacher Folders are pertinent information folders that regular classroom teachers fill out and leave for Substititue Teachers. The folder lists information such as class schedules, classroom procedures, discipline, support personnel, and regular classroom teacher expectations.

Substitute Ingredients
#GP-001

Substitute Ingredients is an informative collection of imaginative language arts, math, and art activities for grades 3 through 8. Reproducible master sheets accompany most activities.

Mastering the Art of Substitute Teaching
#GP-002

Mastering the Art of Substitute Teaching contains many practical ideas for teaching as well as ways to organize activities most effectively. The teaching formats, strategies, and activities are strictly from practical experience.

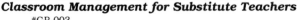

Classroom Management for Substitute Teachers
#GP-003

Classroom Management for Substitute Teachers discusses the substitute teaching role, suggesting procedures for *being-in-charge* in the classroom, establishing rapport, and getting the support of regular classroom teachers and staff.

Lesson Plans for Substitute Teachers
#GP-014

Lesson Plans for a Substitute Teacher is a packet of 15 lesson plan forms. Each form can be easily filled out by regular classroom teachers to provide one day of instruction during their absence.

GARLIC ✿ PRESS / MATH SERIES

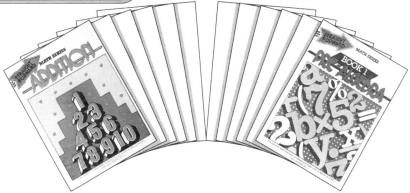

Straight Forward Math Series

Addition #GP-006
Subtraction #GP-012
Multiplication #GP-007
Division #GP-013

The *Straight Forward Math Series* emphasizes mastery of basic math facts – addition, multiplication, subtraction, division.

Each workbook is a simple, straightforward approach to learning a specific mathematical operation. Each workbook is systematic, first diagnosing skill levels, then practice, periodic review, and testing.

Advanced Straight Forward Math Series

Adv. Addition #GP-015
Adv. Subtraction #GP-016
Adv. Multiplication #GP-017
Adv. Division #GP-018
Decimals #GP-020
Fractions #GP-021
Pre-Algebra Book 1 #GP-028
Pre-Algebra Book 2 #GP-029
Pre-Geometry Book 1 #GP-030
Pre-Geometry Book 2 #GP-031

The *Advanced Straight Forward Math Series* picks up where the earlier *Straight Forward Math Series* ends.

SIGN LANGUAGE / HEARING GARLIC ✿ PRESS

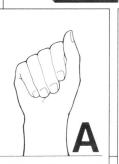

SOUND HEARING
#GP-026

SOUND HEARING provides listening examples to illustrate sound, hearing, and hearing loss. Listeners will hear as impaired people might, listening to music, a story, and taking a simple spelling test. All examples illustrate how hearing can be affected by variables of sound frequency and loudness.

An accompanying booklet provides the script of the audio tape.

A WORD IN THE HAND
#GP-008

A WORD IN THE HAND is a simple, basic primer to Signed English. It contains 15 lessons and nearly 500 illustrations. Each lesson provides vocabulary, illustrations, review, exercises, and assignments that students and adults will find exciting.

SIGN VOCABULARY CARDS
Set A #GP-023, Set B #GP-024

SIGN VOCABULARY CARDS teach simple, basic vocabulary and associated signs. Words have been chosen from basic sight and beginning vocabulary lists to combine with beginning sign language to aid signers in mastering first words and signs.

Two boxed sets, Set A and Set B. 100 words/signs per box. Signed English.

FINGER ALPHABET CARDS
#GP-009

FINGER ALPHABET CARDS are twenty-six sturdy 8 1/2" x 11" cards illustrating the finger alphabet.

These large cards provide the basis for all signing. They provide the beginning signer with the immediate reinforcement that spurs facility in signing.

SIGN NUMBER CARDS
#GP-022

SIGN NUMBER CARDS are 20 sturdy 8 1/2" x 11" cards illustrating numbers 1 to 20. A complement to *FINGER ALPHABET CARDS*, *SIGN NUMBER CARDS* provide beginning signers immediate reinforcement.